COOL APARTMENTS

APPARTEMENTS D'ARCHITECTES

KÖNEMANN

© 2018 koenemann.com GmbH
www.koenemann.com

ÉDITIONS
PLACE DES
VICTOIRES

© Éditions Place des Victoires
6, rue du Mail – 75002 Paris
www.victoires.com
ISBN : 978-2-8099-1641-6
Dépôt légal : 4ᵉ trimestre 2018

Editorial project:
LOFT Publications
Barcelona, Spain
loft@loftpublications.com
www.loftpublications.com

Editorial coordinator:
Claudia Martínez Alonso

Assistant to editorial coordination:
Ana Marques

Edition and texts:
Irene Alegre

Art director:
Mireia Casanovas Soley

Layout:
Sara Abril

Translations:
Textcase

ISBN 978-3-7419-2042-4

Printed in China by Shenzhen Hua Xin Colour-printing & Platemaking Co., Ltd

46 WATER STREET

Omer Arbel/OAO Omer Arbel Office
Vancouver, Canada
© Martin Tessler

This interesting apartment is the result of the renovation of an old warehouse in Gastown's old quarter. The owner wanted an apartment with an open floorplan, in which to enjoy the spaciousness and freedom that a loft offers. The main feature of this property is the inner courtyard, which is only open to the sky and provides natural light to the surrounding rooms.

Dieses interessante Apartment ist das Ergebnis der Sanierung eines alten Lagerhauses im historischen Kern von Gastown. Der Eigentümer wünschte sich eine Wohnung mit einem offenen Raum, in dem er die Weite und die Freiheit genießen kann, die ein Loft bietet. Die große Besonderheit dieser Wohnung besteht aus dem Innenhof, der sich nur zum Himmel hin öffnet und das natürliche Licht in die umliegenden Zimmer leitet.

Cet appartement intéressant est le résultat de la rénovation d'une ancienne boutique située dans la vieille ville de Gastown. Le propriétaire souhaitait un appartement ouvert où il pourrait profiter de l'espace et de la liberté d'un loft. La principale caractéristique de cet appartement réside dans la cour intérieure, qui s'ouvre uniquement vers le ciel et répartit la lumière naturelle dans les pièces qui l'entourent.

Este interesante apartamento es el resultado de la rehabilitación de un antiguo almacén situado en el casco histórico de Gastown. El dueño deseaba tener un piso de planta abierta en el que disfrutar de la amplitud y la libertad que ofrece un *loft*. La principal particularidad de esta vivienda reside en el patio interior, que solo se abre hacia el cielo y reparte la luz natural a las habitaciones que lo rodean.

CHIC ZEN

Fábio Galeazzo
São Paulo, Brazil
© Eduardo Girão

The interior design of this apartment is inspired by the aesthetic tendencies of Zen philosophy. For this reason, pieces of furniture in earth tones were chosen, reminiscent of nature and relaxation. In the middle of the hall, a spectacular eye-shaped chimney presides over the space, and the natural light quality permits the use of darker colours.

Die Innenraumgestaltung dieses Apartments wurde von der Ästhetik der Zen-Philosophie inspiriert. Aus diesem Grund wurden Möbelstücke in Erdtönen ausgewählt, die an die Natur erinnern und dazu einladen, sich zu entspannen. Im Wohnzimmer nimmt der beeindruckende Kamin in Form eines Auges den Mittelpunkt ein und die Qualität des natürlichen Lichts erlaubt den großzügigen Gebrauch dunklerer Farben.

Le projet d'architecture d'intérieur de cet appartement s'inspire des tendances esthétiques de la philosophie zen. Des pièces de mobilier aux tons terre rappellent la nature et invitent à la relaxation. Au milieu du salon, une immense cheminée en forme d'œil domine le séjour, et la qualité de la lumière naturelle permet d'abuser de couleurs plus foncées.

El proyecto de interiorismo de este apartamento se inspira en las tendencias estéticas de la filosofía zen. Por este motivo se han buscado piezas de mobiliario en tonos tierra, que recuerdan a la naturaleza e invitan a la relajación. En el centro del salón, una espectacular chimenea en forma de ojo preside la estancia, y la calidad de la luz natural permite abusar de colores más oscuros.

MATRYOSHKA

Andrea Marcante, Adelaide Testa/UdA Architects
Turin, Italy
© Carola Ripamonti

The layout of this 40 m² post-industrial factory is composed of various boxes, reminiscent of classic Russian dolls. The central module, whose materials and sensory qualities change depending on the time, is the home's main attraction. This is an interesting and versatile feature that adds interest to the day-to-day life of its owners.

Die Wohnung erstreckt sich auf 40 m² über eine postindustrielle Etage und die verschiedenen Verschachtelungen in diesem Apartment erinnern an traditionelle russische Matroschkas. Das zentrale Modul, dessen Materialien und sensorische Qualitäten sich je nach aktueller Funktion ändern, spielt in dieser Wohnung die Hauptrolle. Es ist ein interessantes und vielseitiges Apartment, dass das tagtägliche Leben seiner Eigentümer erleichtert.

Répartis sur les 40 m² d'un appartement postindustriel, les différents « blocs » qui le composent rappellent les célèbres poupées russes. Le module central, dont les matériaux et qualités sensorielles changent selon la fonction du moment, joue le rôle principal de l'appartement. C'est un élément intéressant et polyvalent qui facilite le quotidien de ses propriétaires.

Distribuidas en los 40 m² de una planta postindustrial, las distintas cajas que forman este apartamento recuerdan a las clásicas muñecas rusas. El módulo central, cuyos materiales y cualidades sensoriales cambian dependiendo de la función del momento, es el gran protagonista de la vivienda. Se trata de un elemento interesante y polivalente que resuelve el día a día de sus propietarios.

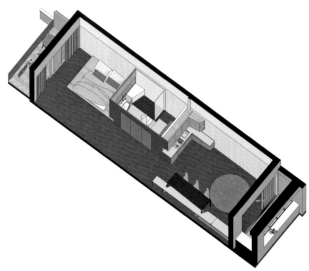

Axonometric view

FUN HOUSE

Andrea Marcante, Adelaide Testa/UdA Architects
Juan-les-Pins, France
© Carola Ripamonti

In a 1960s coastal building, this apartment of just 40 m² houses two bedrooms and a spacious relaxation area. Inspired by the Italian communes of a few decades ago, the home is designed to be enjoyed by two families at a time. The metal and wooden dividers generate differentiated spaces and the colours reflect nature.

Dieses nur 40 m² große Apartment aus den sechziger Jahren befindet sich an der Küste und hat zwei Schlafzimmer und einen weitläufigen Erholungsbereich. Es ist von den italienischen Kommunen inspiriert, die es vor ein paar Jahrzehnten gab und die Wohnung wurde so entworfen, dass hier zwei Familien gleichzeitig wohnen können. Die Trennwände aus Holz und Metall unterteilen die Räume und ihre Farbe spiegelt die Natur wieder.

Situé dans un édifice côtier des années 1960, cet appartement de 40 m² est composé de deux chambres et d'une spacieuse pièce de détente. Inspirée des villes italiennes d'il y a quelques décennies, l'habitation est conçue pour accueillir deux familles. Les séparations en métal et en bois créent des espaces indépendants. La couleur reflète la nature.

Emplazado en un edificio costero de los años sesenta, este apartamento de tan solo 40 m² contiene en su interior dos dormitorios y una espaciosa área de relajación. Inspirada en las comunas italianas de hace unas décadas, la vivienda está diseñada para que la disfruten dos familias a la vez. Los separadores de metal y madera generan espacios diferenciados y el color refleja la naturaleza.

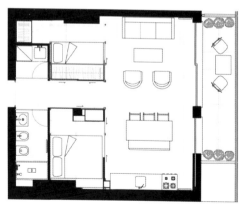

Floor plan

TRIBECA NY

Valerie Pasquiou Interiors & Design
New York, NY, USA
© Véronique Mati

This loft, where the designer is also the owner, is the result of a fun, original and somewhat eclectic interior design project. There are spaces and elements of diverse origin along the length and width of the open floorplan: small cosy corners, antique furniture, yellow chairs and a spectacular window that illuminates the entire house.

Dieses Loft, dessen Eigentümerin auch gleichzeitig die Designerin ist, ist das Ergebnis eines farbenfrohen, originellen und etwas eklektischen Inneneinrichtungsprojekts. Über die gesamte Länge und Breite des offenen Stockwerks verteilt erstrecken sich Räume und Elemente verschiedensten Ursprungs: kleine und gemütliche Ecken, antikes Mobiliar, gelbe Stühle und ein spektakuläres Fenster, das die gesamte Wohnung beleuchtet.

Ce loft, dont l'architecte en est également la propriétaire, est le résultat d'un projet original, drôle et quelque peu éclectique. Les espaces et éléments de diverses origines sont répartis dans l'appartement ouvert : petits recoins accueillants, mobilier ancien, chaises jaunes et grandes fenêtres qui illuminent toute l'habitation.

Este *loft*, del que la diseñadora es también propietaria, es el resultado de un proyecto de interiorismo divertido, original y algo ecléctico. A lo largo y ancho de la planta abierta se distribuyen espacios y elementos de origen diverso: rincones pequeños y acogedores, mobiliario antiguo, sillas de color amarillo y un espectacular ventanal que ilumina toda la vivienda.

Une petite plume s'est égarée.
Au gré du vent, elle a dansé.
Par la fenêtre, elle est entrée
et sur mon mur, elle s'est posée.

SH

Valerie Pasquiou Interiors & Design
New York, NY, USA
© Antonie Bootz, Costa Picadas

Sue Hostetler, editor-in-chief of the journal *Art Basel Miami Beach* lives in this apartment. The interior design reflects the personality of its owner and consists of a blend of mid-20th-century modernist pieces and traditional furniture. Natural light penetrates the different rooms in this elegant, modern and welcoming home.

In dieser Wohnung lebt Sue Hostetler, die Chefredakteurin der Zeitschrift *Art Basel Miami Beach*. Das Inneneinrichtungsprojekt spiegelt die Persönlichkeit der Eigentümerin wieder und besteht aus einer Mischung aus modernen Möbelstücken aus der Mitte des 20. Jahrhunderts und traditionellen Möbeln. Das natürliche Licht durchflutet die verschiedenen Zimmer dieser eleganten, modernen und gemütlichen Wohnung.

Cet appartement est la résidence de Sue Hostetler, rédactrice en chef du magazine *Art Basel Miami Beach*. Le projet d'intérieur reflète la personnalité de la propriétaire : on y trouve un mélange de pièces modernes du milieu du XXe siècle et de mobilier traditionnel. La lumière naturelle envahit les différentes pièces de cette habitation élégante, moderne et accueillante.

En este apartamento vive Sue Hostetler, la redactora jefa de la revista *Art Basel Miami Beach*. El proyecto de interiorismo refleja la personalidad de su propietaria y consiste en una mezcla de piezas modernistas de mediados del siglo XX y mobiliario tradicional. La luz natural invade las distintas habitaciones de esta vivienda elegante, moderna y acogedora.

LOVEBIRD APARTMENT

Nomade Architettura e Interior Design
Milan, Italy
© Deniz Şiar Bozkut

In the heart of the city, this small and cosy apartment reflects the personality of its owners. The décor consists of a mixture of provincial-style features with a touch of contemporary modernity that provides the home with warmth and originality. The birds figurine is a nod to the name of the project, designed for a young couple.

Dieses kleine und gemütliche Apartment mitten in der Stadt spiegelt die Persönlichkeit seiner Eigentümer wieder. Die Dekoration besteht aus einer Mischung aus Vintage- Elementen und Elementen, die mit einem modernen, zeitgenössischen Touch Wärme und Originalität in die Wohnung bringen. Die kleine Vogelfigur ist eine Anspielung auf den Namen des Projekts, das für ein junges Paar erdacht wurde.

Ce petit appartement accueillant, situé au cœur de la ville, reflète la personnalité de ses propriétaires. La décoration est un mélange d'éléments de style providentiel et d'une touche de modernité contemporaine qui apportent au logement chaleur et originalité. La représentation des couples est un clin d'œil du projet, imaginé pour un jeune couple.

Este pequeño y acogedor apartamento, situado en el corazón de la ciudad, refleja la personalidad de sus propietarios. La decoración consiste en una mezcla de elementos de estilo providencial y un toque de modernidad contemporánea que proporcionan a la vivienda calidez y originalidad. La figurita de los pájaros es un guiño al nombre del proyecto, ideado para una joven pareja.

APARTMENT IN MILAN

Nomade Architettura e Interior Design
Milan, Italy
© Deniz Şiar Bozkut

Colourful, recycled, decorative features have been incorporated into this small apartment that surprises visitors and brings a smile to their faces. Retro taste is expressed with a mixture of objects, ranging from old briefcases and curious wrought iron cages to the classic Campbell's tomato soup cans.

In diesem Mini-Apartment wurden dekorative, recycelte und gefärbte Elemente eingebaut, die Besucher überraschen und ihnen garantiert ein Lächeln entlocken. Der Hang zum Retro zeigt sich in einer Mischung aus Objekten, die von alten Koffern und witzigen schmiedeeisernen Vogelkäfigen, bis hin zu den klassischen Campbell-Tomatendosen reicht.

Cet appartement à la surface réduite a été rehaussé d'éléments décoratifs recyclés et colorés qui surprennent et font sourire les visiteurs. Le goût rétro s'impose dans un mélange d'objets tels que des anciennes malles et d'étranges cages en fer forgé, ou encore les classiques boîtes de conserve de tomates de la marque Campbell's.

En este apartamento de reducidas dimensiones se han incorporado elementos decorativos reciclados y coloridos que sorprenden al visitante y logran sacarle una sonrisa. El gusto por lo retro se impone en una mezcla de objetos que van desde los maletines antiguos y las curiosas jaulas de hierro forjado, a las clásicas latas de tomate Campbell's.

REAL PARQUE LOFT

Diego Revollo
São Paulo, Brazil
© Alain Brugier

This loft is based on a remodel where many of the apartment's original walls were torn down, opening out the floorplan and gaining a great feeling of spaciousness. The union of cement and natural wood in shades of red, as well as the choice of fabrics, brings warmth to the space. The result is a home without excesses – spacious and perfect to live in.

Dieses Loft entstand aus einem Umbau, bei dem viele Wände des ursprünglichen Apartments herausgerissen wurden und aus dem so ein Stockwerk entstand, das einen Eindruck von Weite vermittelt. Das Zusammenspiel von Zement und Naturholz in Rottönen, sowie die Auswahl der Heimtextilien, bringen Wärme in den Raum. Das Ergebnis ist eine schlichte Wohnung, die geräumig und perfekt zum Leben geeignet ist.

Ce loft est le résultat d'une rénovation lors de laquelle les nombreuses cloisons de l'appartement d'origine ont été supprimées pour ouvrir l'espace et renforcer la sensation d'espace. Le mariage du ciment et du bois naturel aux tons rougeâtres, ainsi que le choix des tissus, apportent une certaine chaleur. Il en résulte un lieu de vie parfait, spacieux et sans excès.

Este *loft* deriva de una reforma que tiró abajo las numerosas paredes del apartamento original y abrió la planta, con lo que se obtuvo una gran sensación de amplitud. La unión del cemento y la madera natural en tonos rojizos, así como la elección de los tejidos del hogar, aporta calidez al espacio. El resultado es una vivienda sin excesos, espaciosa y perfecta para vivir.

CHOY RESIDENCE

HEAD Architecture and Design
Hong Kong, China
© HEAD Architecture and Design

This 288 m² duplex has been converted into a loft with a lounge, dining room, kitchen, two children's bedrooms with bathroom and a multimedia room on the first floor. The main bedroom is on the second floor, with access to a bathroom with views over the bay. On the rooftop, the open floor plan includes a Jacuzzi and an outdoor cinema.

Diese 288 m² große Maisonette-Wohnung wurde zu einem Loft umgestaltet und im ersten Stockwerk mit einem Wohnzimmer, einem Esszimmer, einer Küche, zwei Kinderzimmern mit Bad und einem Multimedia-Raum ausgestattet. Im zweiten Stockwerk befindet sich das Hauptschlafzimmer mit Zugang zum Bad mit Ausblick auf die Bucht. Auf der Dachterrasse ist ein offener Bereich mit Whirlpool und Open-Air-Kino untergebracht.

Ce duplex de 288 m² a été transformé en loft. Le rez-de-chaussée accueille un salon, une salle à manger, une cuisine, deux chambres pour enfants avec salle de bains et une salle multimédia. À l'étage se trouve la chambre principale avec une salle de bain offrant une vue sur la baie. La terrasse permet de profiter d'un jacuzzi et d'un cinéma de plein air.

Este dúplex de 288 m² se ha reconvertido en *loft* con un salón, un comedor, una cocina, dos habitaciones infantiles con cuarto de baño y una sala multimedia en la primera planta. En el segundo piso se encuentra el dormitorio principal, con acceso a un cuarto de baño con vistas a la bahía. En la azotea, la planta abierta acomoda un hidromasaje y un cine al aire libre.

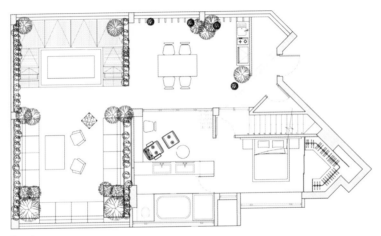

Floor plan

APARTMENT FOR IRENE

Olga Akulova DESIGN
Kiev, Ukraine
© Roman Shishak

Located in the city centre, this 200 m^2 apartment has two floors and two terraces, from which you can see Maidan Square. The interior colour range of warm and classic hues, which covers the architectural structure, contrasts with the accents of colour provided by some of the furniture pieces. The spiral staircase has become the home's main focus.

Dieses 200 m^2 große Apartment befindet sich im Stadtzentrum und hat zwei Stockwerke und zwei Terrassen, von denen aus man den Platz Maidán sehen kann. Im Innenraum herrscht eine monochrome Farbpalette in warmen und klassischen Tönen vor, die die architektonische Struktur verdecken und die im Kontrast mit den Farbtönen einiger Möbelstücke stehen. Die Wendeltreppe ist das Hauptelement dieser Wohnung.

Situé en plein cœur de la ville, cet appartement de 200 m^2 compte deux niveaux et deux terrasses qui donnent sur la Place de l'Indépendance. À l'intérieur, la gamme chromatique aux tons chauds et classiques qui couvrent la structure architectonique contraste avec les touches de couleurs de quelques pièces de mobilier. L'escalier en colimaçon joue un rôle central dans l'appartement.

Situado en el centro de la ciudad, este apartamento de 200 m^2 cuenta con dos plantas y dos terrazas desde las que se puede ver la plaza Maidán. En su interior, la gama cromática en tonos cálidos y clásicos que cubre la estructura arquitectónica contrasta con las notas de color en algunas de las piezas de mobiliario. La escalera de caracol se convierte en la protagonista de la vivienda.

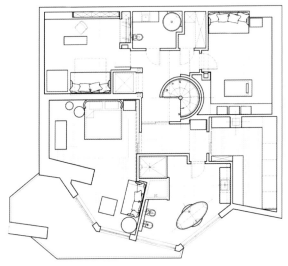

Second floor plan

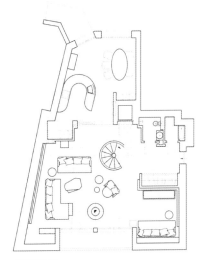

First floor plan

MORGAGNI FLAT

Selina Bertola/Nomade Architettura e Interior Design
Milan, Italy
© Nomade Architettura e Interior Design

This home, with the traditional layout of a 1930s Milanese apartment, was remodelled in 2012. The refinement of the floors, window frames and doors contrasts with the clean, sharp lines of the furniture design. The lounge and dining room are joined by a wide passage that increases the feeling of spaciousness.

Diese Wohnung stellt die traditionelle Aufteilung der Mailänder Apartments in den dreißiger Jahren dar und wurde 2012 umgebaut. Die raffinierten Böden, die Fensterrahmen und die Türen kontrastieren mit dem Design der Möbel, die schlichte und spitze Linien haben. Das Wohnzimmer und das Esszimmer sind durch einen breiten Flur miteinander verbunden, der das Gefühl von Weite verstärkt.

Cet appartement, à la disposition traditionnelle milanaise des années 1930, a été rénové en 2012. L'amélioration du plancher et les encadrements des fenêtres et des portes contrastent avec le mobilier, aux lignes simples et fines. Le salon et la salle à manger sont réunis par un large couloir qui renforce la sensation de volume.

Este piso, que presenta la distribución tradicional de los apartamentos milaneses de los años treinta, fue remodelado en el 2012. El refinamiento de los suelos, los marcos de las ventanas y las puertas contrastan con el diseño del mobiliario, de líneas simples y afiladas. El salón y el comedor se unen mediante un ancho pasillo que aumenta la sensación de amplitud.

RUTHERFORD APARTMENT

Carretero Design
New York, NY, USA
© Jacob Sadrak

With textured surfaces and a masculine, made-to-measure style the design of this apartment reinvents the traditional layout of a small home and creates different areas with personality and character, which together provide a feeling of openness and space. The various pieces of furniture are attractive and functional and make the apartment a home with timeless style.

Mit seinen strukturierten Oberflächen und in einem weitgehend maskulinen Stil gehalten, erfindet das Design dieses Apartments die traditionelle Aufteilung einer kleinen Wohnung neu und schafft vielseitige Bereiche mit Persönlichkeit und Charakter, die ein Gefühl von Raum und Weite geben. Die unterschiedlichen Möbelstücke sehen gut aus, sind praktisch und verwandeln das Apartment in ein zeitloses Zuhause.

Avec des surfaces à texture et un style masculin et sur mesure, la conception de cet appartement réinvente la répartition traditionnelle d'un petit logement. Les différentes pièces créées révèlent chacune une personnalité et un caractère qui apportent une sensation d'espace et de profondeur. Les éléments de mobilier offrent charme et fonctionnalité et transforment l'appartement en habitation au style intemporel.

Con superficies texturizadas y un estilo masculino y a medida, el diseño de este apartamento reinventa la distribución tradicional de una vivienda pequeña y crea distintas áreas con personalidad y carácter que en su conjunto proporcionan sensación de espacio y amplitud. Las diferentes piezas de mobiliario son atractivas y funcionales y convierten el piso en un hogar de estilo atemporal.

MC APARTMENT REFURBISHMENT

Vaillo & Irigaray, Íñigo Beguiristáin
Pamplona, Spain
© Iñaki Bergera

A new scale of almost palatial dimensions has been introduced into this home. Theatrical imagery was added to this structure with heavy curtains as the main feature, crossing the whole space, morphing backgrounds and obscuring the linear continuity of the structure. Neutral colours give the décor a sober touch.

Diese Wohnung erreicht mit fast palastartigen Ausmaßen eine neue Dimension. Die Struktur ist an eine theatralische Ikonografie gekoppelt, bei der die schweren Vorhänge, die im gesamten Raum angebracht wurden, die Hauptrolle spielen. Sie verstecken Hintergründe und verwischen die Kontinuität der Linien. Die neutralen Farben lassen die Dekoration dennoch schlicht wirken.

Une nouvelle échelle de dimensions presque comparable à celles d'un palais a été introduite dans cet appartement. À la structure s'ajoute l'emploi d'une iconographie théâtrale remplie par les lourds rideaux qui longent tout l'espace, modifient l'arrière-plan et estompent la continuité des lignes. Les couleurs neutres confèrent une certaine sobriété à la décoration.

En esta vivienda se ha introducido una nueva escala de dimensiones casi palaciegas. A la estructura se le suma la utilización de una iconografía teatral protagonizada por las pesadas cortinas que recorren la totalidad del espacio, desfiguran fondos y difuminan la continuidad de las líneas. Los colores neutros proporcionan sobriedad a la decoración.

Floor plan

GRAMERCY TOWNHOUSE

Fractal Construction
New York, NY, USA
© Eric Laignel

The remodelling of this dwelling began with the introduction of a new steel structure and the replacement of electrical installations and plumbing. The ceilings in the living room and kitchen are sculpted with light sources that create constellations, and sculptures have been hung from them that comply with the function of a lamp. The roof has become a garden terrace.

Der Umbau dieser Wohnung begann mit der Einführung einer neuen Stahlkonstruktion und der Erneuerung der gesamten Elektrik und der Rohre. Die Decken des Wohnzimmers und der Küche wurden mit Lichtquellen gestaltet, die Konstellationen zeichnen und von denen Skulpturen herabhängen, die als Lampen funktionieren. Das Dach wurde in eine begrünte Terrasse verwandelt.

La rénovation de cet appartement a commencé par l'ajout d'une nouvelle structure en acier et le remplacement de l'installation électrique et de la plomberie. Le plafond du salon et de la cuisine est sculpté avec des sources de lumière qui forment des constellations. Des sculptures y sont accrochées pour jouer le rôle de luminaire. Le toit a été aménagé en terrasse avec espaces verts.

La reforma de esta vivienda comenzó con la introducción de una nueva estructura de acero y el reemplazo de la instalación eléctrica y la fontanería. Los techos del salón y la cocina están esculpidos con fuentes de luz que dibujan constelaciones, y de ellos cuelgan esculturas que cumplen con la función de una lámpara. El tejado se ha convertido en una terraza ajardinada.

LOFT GRAND STREET

Labo Design Studio
New York, NY, USA
© Jean Bourbon

The renovation of this loft transformed a cramped apartment into a spacious home, full of light. The project proposes a new transition system of spaces that flow naturally. The blackened steel kitchen, together with the shelving and wardrobe, emphasize the loft concept. The industrial aesthetic is preserved by using a monochrome palette.

Die Renovierung dieses Lofts verwandelte ein Apartment, das ursprünglich überfüllt war, in eine weite Wohnung voller Licht. Das Projekt schafft neue Übergänge zwischen den Räumen, die natürlich zu fließen scheinen. Die geschwärzte Stahlküche, zusammen mit den Regalen und dem Schrank, betonen das Loft-Konzept. Die einheitliche Farbpalette bewahrt die Industrieästhetik.

La rénovation de ce loft a permis de transformer un appartement à l'origine surchargé en une habitation spacieuse et lumineuse. Le projet propose un nouveau système de transition des espaces qui s'écoule naturellement. La cuisine en acier noirci, ainsi que les étagères et l'armoire, soulignent le concept de loft. La palette monochromatique conserve l'esthétique industrielle.

La renovación de este *loft* transformó un apartamento originariamente abarrotado en una vivienda amplia y llena de luz. El proyecto propone un nuevo sistema de transición de espacios que fluye de forma natural. La cocina de acero ennegrecido, junto con la estantería y el armario, enfatiza el concepto de *loft*. La paleta monocromática conserva la estética industrial.

BOXING LIFE

Andrea Marcante, Adelaide Testa/UdA Architects
Turin, Italy
© Carola Ripamonti, Stefano Graziani

Like a Chinese box puzzle, a neighbourhood contains a building, which contains an apartment. Inside, a room contains furniture, and inside this there are objects to be found. The dimensions of the features are reduced but their value prevails. There are contrasting pieces: metal surfaces and hand-lacquered wood, and polished edges alongside rough-textured materials. A paradoxical apartment.

Wie beim Spiel der chinesischen Schachteln steht hier ein Gebäude in einem Stadtteil und darin befindet sich ein Apartment. In seinem Inneren stehen Möbel in einem Zimmer und in diesen findet man Objekte. Die Größe der Elemente ist reduziert, aber ihr Wert bleibt gleich. Die Stücke stehen im Gegensatz zueinander: Metalloberflächen treffen auf von Hand lackiertes Holz und polierte Kanten ergänzen Materialien mit groben Strukturen. Ein Apartment mit vielen Widersprüchen.

Comme dans le jeu des boîtes chinoises, un quartier accueille un bâtiment qui accueille un appartement. À l'intérieur, une habitation accueille des meubles, lesquels abritent des objets. Les différents éléments sont de plus en plus petits, leur valeur va crescendo. Tout s'oppose : surfaces métalliques et bois laqué, bords polis et matières aux textures rugueuses. Un appartement paradoxal.

Como en el juego de las cajas chinas, un barrio contiene un edificio que contiene un apartamento. En su interior, una habitación contiene muebles, y en estos se encuentran los objetos. Las dimensiones de los elementos se reducen pero su valor prevalece. Las piezas se contraponen: superficies metálicas y madera lacada a mano o cantos pulidos junto a materiales de texturas rugosas. Un apartamento paradójico.

First floor plan

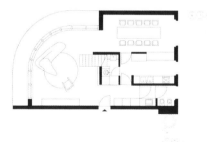

Second floor plan

ULTRA LUXURY APARTMENT

Pablo Jendretzki/JENDRETZKI LLC
New York, NY, USA
© Alejandro Wirth Photo

This Park Avenue home was designed to provide serenity and relaxation for its owners. This effect is achieved with the use of minimalist lines and natural materials. Light penetrates the dining room through wooden slatted panels that can be separated to create a single open space.

Diese Wohnung liegt an der Park Avenue und wurde mit dem Ziel entworfen, ihren Eigentümern Gelassenheit und Entspannung zu bieten. Dieser Effekt wird durch den Gebrauch minimalistischer Linien und natürlicher Materialien erzielt. Das Licht fällt durch vorgefertigte Platten aus Holzlatten in das Esszimmer, die Platten kann man trennen und so einen einzigen, offenen Raum schaffen.

Situé sur Park Avenue, cet appartement a été conçu dans le but d'apporter calme et sérénité à ses propriétaires. L'objectif est atteint grâce à l'emploi de lignes minimalistes et de matières naturelles. La lumière pénètre dans la salle à manger par des panneaux fabriqués avec des lattes de bois, pouvant être ouverts pour créer un espace unique.

Situada en Park Avenue, esta vivienda fue diseñada con el objetivo de proporcionar serenidad y descanso a sus propietarios. El efecto se logra con el uso de líneas minimalistas y materiales naturales. La luz penetra en el comedor a través de paneles fabricados con listones de madera que pueden separarse para crear un único espacio abierto.

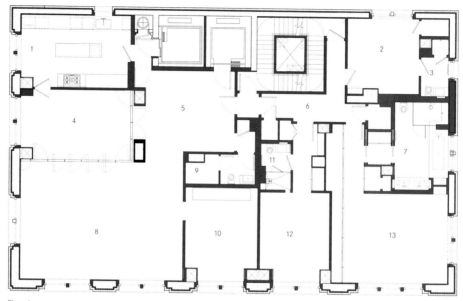

Floor plan

1. Kitchen
2. Bedroom 2
3. Bath 2
4. Dining room
5. Foyer
6. Bedroom hallway
7. Master bath
8. Living room
9. Powder room
10. Library
11. Bath 3
12. Bedroom 3
13. Master bedroom

SOUTH BEACH PENTHOUSE

Oppenheim Architecture + Design
Miami, FL, USA
© Laziz Hamani

Designed for the retired chairman of a Latin American television channel, this two-storey penthouse exhibits a luxurious and minimalist style. Twenty-six televisions are strategically placed on the interior teak and shagreen walls. The space is reduced down to its essence and has only two bedrooms, one of them divided into two floors connected by a staircase.

Dieses Penthaus auf zwei Ebenen wurde für den in Rente gegangenen Präsidenten eines lateinamerikanischen Fernsehsenders entworfen und ist in einem luxuriösen und minimalistischen Stil gehalten. Sechsundzwanzig Fernseher wurden strategisch in die Wände aus Teakholz und Chagrin eingelassen. Der Raum ist aufs Wesentliche reduziert und es gibt nur zwei Schlafzimmer. Eins davon ist über zwei Etagen aufgeteilt, die mit einer Treppe miteinander verbunden sind.

Conçu pour le président retraité d'une chaîne de télévision latino-américaine, cet attique sur deux niveaux affiche un style luxueux et minimaliste. Vingt-six téléviseurs sont stratégiquement placés dans les parois en teck et noyer. L'espace est réduit à l'essentiel : on trouve deux chambres, dont l'une occupe les deux niveaux, et dont les deux parties sont reliées par un escalier.

Diseñado para el presidente ya retirado de una televisión latinoamericana, este ático de dos plantas exhibe un estilismo lujoso y minimalista. Veintiséis televisores están estratégicamente colocados en el interior de las paredes de teca y chagrín. El espacio se reduce a su esencia y cuenta solamente con dos dormitorios, uno de ellos repartido entre dos plantas conectadas por una escalera.

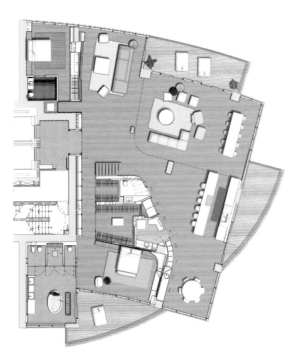

First floor plan

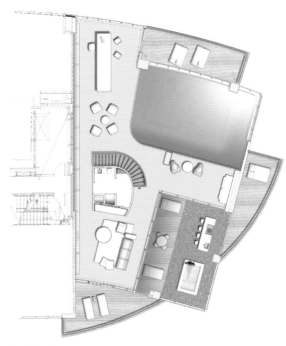

Second floor plan

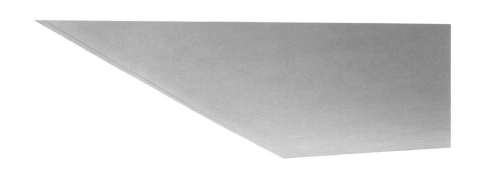

LIVING BY THE MARKET

Daniel Pérez, Felipe Araujo/Egue y Seta
Barcelona, Spain
© Víctor Hugo, Mauricio Fuertes

Located near the Santa Caterina market, this apartment is an attempt to return to the roots of the traditional apartment. Its interior design features local components that intersect with new lifestyles. The result is a contemporary dwelling that avoids transitional spaces and successfully increases the general feeling of spaciousness as well as the propagation of light.

Dieses Apartment liegt in der Nähe des Santa Caterina Markts und beruft sich auf die Wurzeln der traditionellen Apartments hier. Die Gestaltung des Interieurs besteht aus landestypischen Elementen, die sich mit neuen Lebensformen verflechten. Das Ergebnis ist eine zeitgenössische Wohnung ohne Übergangsräume, die das Gefühl der allgemeinen Weite vermittelt und viel Licht hineinlässt.

Situé à proximité du marché de Sainte-Catherine, cet appartement tente de retourner aux racines de l'appartement traditionnel. Sa conception intérieure comporte des éléments vernaculaires qui se mêlent aux nouveaux styles de vie. Le résultat en est une habitation contemporaine qui évite les espaces de transition et parvient à augmenter la sensation d'espace et la diffusion de lumière.

Situado cerca del mercado de Santa Caterina, este apartamento intenta volver a las raíces del apartamento tradicional. Su diseño de interiores cuenta con elementos vernáculos que se entrelazan con las nuevas formas de vivir. El resultado es una vivienda contemporánea que evita los espacios de transición y consigue aumentar la sensación de amplitud general y la propagación de la luz.

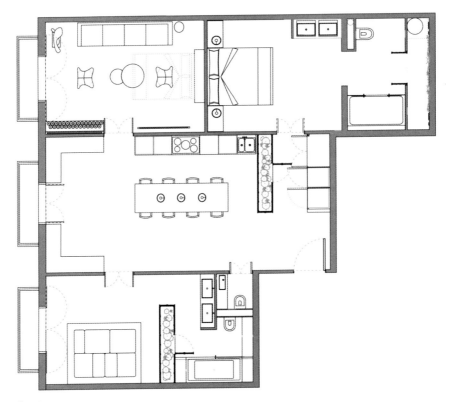

Floor plan

PRIVATE APARTMENT MM

TOP TAG Milano
Milan, Italy
© Marco Curatolo

The design of this apartment is based on a 6-metre-long glass wall. The lounge is designed as a single space, bathed in light from the large window. A low divider separates it from the kitchen and provides storage areas at the same time. The made-to-measure furniture maximises the use of every square metre.

Das Design dieser Wohnung geht von einer 6 Meter langen Glaswand aus. Das Wohnzimmer ist ein einzigartiger Raum, der durch die großen Fenster mit Licht durchflutet wird. Eine niedrige Trennwand trennt es von der Küche und bietet gleichzeitig Stauraum. Die maßgefertigten Möbel nutzen jeden Quadratzentimeter optimal aus.

La conception de cet appartement est née d'une baie vitrée de 6 mètres de long. Le salon est conçu comme un espace unique inondé de lumière qui pénètre par la grande baie vitrée. Un élément de séparation à faible hauteur le coupe de la cuisine et offre des espaces de rangement. Le mobilier fabriqué sur mesure optimise chaque mètre carré.

El diseño de este apartamento parte de una pared de cristal de 6 metros de largo. El salón se concibe como un espacio único inundado de la luz que atraviesa el gran ventanal. Un divisor de baja altura lo separa de la cocina y, a la vez, proporciona zonas de almacenaje. El mobiliario fabricado a medida aprovecha al máximo cada metro cuadrado.

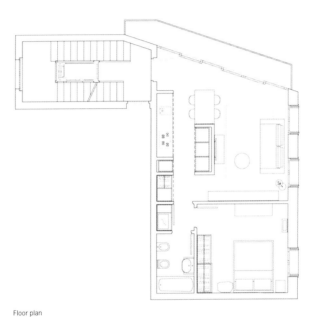

Floor plan

JOSÉ ORTEGA Y GASSET

Beriot, Bernardini Arquitectos
Madrid, Spain
© Yen Chen

This renovation project has retained the ceiling mouldings in the daytime area. The 200 m² apartment has an open floorplan that offers a unique space dedicated to the living room, dining room and kitchen. The layout of the rest of the house is simple and functional, leaving the two bathrooms and dressing room as a preface to the master bedroom.

Bei diesem Renovierungsprojekt wurde die Deckenform im Tagesbereich beibehalten. Das 200 m² große Apartment besitzt ein offenes Stockwerk, mit nur einem Raum, der als Wohnzimmer, Esszimmer und Küche dient. Der Rest der Wohnung verteilt sich auf einfache und funktionale Weise und die beiden Bäder und das Ankleidezimmer sind sozusagen die Präambel zum Hauptschlafzimmer.

Ce projet de rénovation conserve les moulures au plafond des pièces de vie. L'appartement de 200 m² est composé d'un rez-de-chaussée ouvert qui offre un espace unique dédié au salon, à la salle à manger et à la cuisine. Le reste de l'habitation est réparti de manière simple et fonctionnelle : deux salles de bains et un vestiaire sont accolés à la chambre principale.

Este proyecto de renovación conserva las molduras del techo en el área diurna. El apartamento, de 200 m², cuenta con una planta abierta que ofrece un único espacio dedicado a salón, comedor y cocina. El resto de la vivienda se distribuye de un modo simple y funcional que deja los dos baños y el vestidor como preámbulo del dormitorio principal.

CHET BAKERSTRAAT

Barbara Dujardin, Michiel Hofman,
Nuno Urbano/HofmanDujardin
Amsterdam, the Netherlands
© Matthijs van Roon

This property has been completely renovated. A new layout was designed, changing the materials and introducing a new lighting scheme. The kitchen has been integrated in the living room. The oversized furniture generates a feeling of intimacy and visually connects spaces, while light and neutral colours add a touch of modernity and warmth.

Diese Wohnung wurde komplett renoviert. Es wurde eine neue Aufteilung gewählt, Materialien ausgetauscht und ein neues Beleuchtungsschema eingeführt. Die Küche wurde ins Wohnzimmer integriert. Die großen Möbel schaffen den Eindruck von Intimität und verbinden optisch die Räume miteinander, während die hellen und neutralen Farben einen Touch Modernität und Wärme hinzufügen.

Cette habitation a été entièrement rénovée. Une nouvelle répartition a été proposée, les matériaux ont été changés et un nouveau plan d'éclairage a été installé. La cuisine a été intégrée au salon. Les meubles de grande taille créent une sensation d'intimité et relient visuellement les différents espaces, tandis que les couleurs claires et neutres apportent une touche de modernité et de chaleur.

Esta vivienda ha sido totalmente renovada. Se propuso una nueva distribución, se cambiaron los materiales y se introdujo un nuevo esquema de iluminación. La cocina se ha integrado en el salón. Los muebles de gran tamaño generan sensación de intimidad y conectan visualmente los espacios, mientras que los colores claros y neutros aportan un toque de modernidad y calidez.

Floor plan

APARTMENT FOR AN ART COLLECTOR

Ricardo Salvi, Luca Rossire / Logica:architettura
Milan, Italy
© Simone Colombo

Inspired by Milanese design from the late fifties and early sixties, this apartment, in the centre of the metropolis, was designed for an art collector. The home is comfortable, cosy and functional at the same time. The amalgam of styles is fascinating and the interior design exudes a refined interest in the detail of the forms and textures.

Inspiriert von den Kreationen der Mailänder Schule der fünfziger und sechziger Jahre, wurde diese Wohnung mitten in der Metropole für einen Kunstsammler entworfen. Die Wohnung ist bequem, gemütlich und gleichzeitig funktional. Die Mischung der Stile ist faszinierend und das Innengestaltungsprojekt strahlt ein raffiniertes Interesse am Detail der Formen und Texturen aus.

Inspiré des créations de l'école milanaise des années 1950 et 1960, cet appartement situé au centre de la métropole a été conçu par un collectionneur d'art. L'habitation est à la fois confortable, accueillante et fonctionnelle. Le mélange des styles s'avère fascinant et le projet d'architecture d'intérieur dénote un intérêt raffiné pour le détail des textures et des formes.

Inspirado en las creaciones de la escuela milanesa de los años cincuenta y sesenta, este apartamento situado en el centro de la metrópoli se diseñó para un coleccionista de arte. La vivienda es cómoda, acogedora y funcional a la vez. La amalgama de estilos resulta fascinante y el proyecto de interiorismo destila un refinado interés por el detalle de las formas y las texturas.

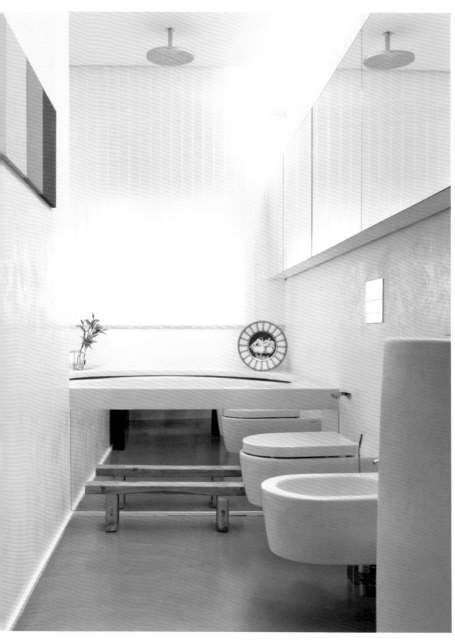

TTMNT

Najmias Oficina de Arquitectura (NOA)
Buenos Aires, Argentina
© Najmias Oficina de Arquitectura (NOA)

The undisputed protagonist of this apartment is the kitchen table, an almost sculptural piece. With structure and gravity as the project's central themes, the surface "floats" in the middle of the space. To achieve this effect, the design has different thicknesses that energise the geometric lines of the central piece of furniture.

Die Hauptrolle in diesem Apartment nimmt ohne Frage der Küchentisch ein, er ist beinah ein Kunstwerk für sich. Mit der Struktur und der Schwerkraft als zentrale Themen des Projekts, „schwebt" die Oberfläche mitten im Raum. Um diesen Effekt zu erreichen, spielt das Design mit verschiedenen Dicken, die den geometrischen Linien des Tischs als zentralem Möbelstück Dynamik geben.

La table de la cuisine, qui peut être comparée à une sculpture, joue indéniablement le rôle principal dans cet appartement. Les thèmes principaux du projet étant la structure et la gravitation, la surface « flotte » au milieu de l'espace. Pour obtenir cet effet, l'architecte joue avec des épaisseurs différentes qui dynamisent les lignes géométriques de la pièce de mobilier centrale.

La indiscutible protagonista de este apartamento es la mesa de la cocina, una pieza casi escultórica. Con la estructura y la gravedad como temas centrales del proyecto, la superficie «flota» en medio del espacio. Para lograr este efecto, el diseño cuenta con distintos grosores que dinamizan las líneas geométricas de la pieza de mobiliario central.

ILARIA'S APARTMENT

Macmamau
Pescara, Italy
© Sergio Camplone

In this small duplex, the designer uses different solutions and made-to-measure furniture to optimise the use of the various spaces. The kitchen, the shelving and the wardrobe fit perfectly into their respective corners. Brilliant white finishes were chosen to reflect light and provide a sense of spaciousness.

In diesem kleinen Duplex nutzt der Designer die verschiedenen Räume mit maßgefertigten Lösungen und Möbeln maximal. Die Küche, die Regale und der Schrank passen sich perfekt an ihre jeweilige Umgebung an. Die weißen Hochglanz-Oberflächen reflektieren das Licht und vermitteln einen Eindruck von Weite.

Dans ce petit duplex, l'architecte exploite au maximum les différentes pièces avec des solutions et du mobilier conçus sur mesure. La cuisine, les étagères et l'armoire s'adaptent parfaitement à leurs espaces respectifs. Les finitions en blanc brillant ont été choisies pour refléter la lumière et apporter une sensation de volume.

En este pequeño dúplex, el diseñador aprovecha al máximo los distintos espacios con soluciones y mobiliario fabricados a medida. La cocina, las estanterías y el armario se adaptan perfectamente a sus respectivos rincones. Se han elegido acabados en blanco brillante, que refleja la luz y proporciona sensación de amplitud.

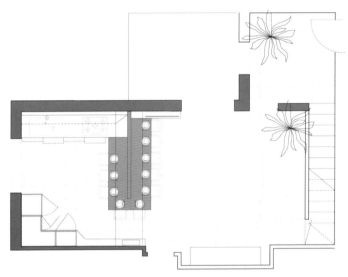

Floor plan

GAUER GOLDSMITH APARTMENT

James Gauer architecture + design
Victoria, Canada
© Peter Joshua Lawrence

This 116 m² apartment is divided into four spatial layers that invigorate and provide depth. In the first layer, there is a foyer reception area. The passage crosses the pantry, the bathrooms and the kitchen. In the third zone, the bedroom and the living room revel in their spaciousness. On the horizon, the terrace forms the fourth layer.

Diese Wohnung ist in vier räumliche Ebenen unterteilt, die Dynamik und Tiefe schaffen und ist insgesamt 116 m² groß. In der ersten Ebene werden Besucher im *Foyer* empfangen. Auf dem Weg zur dritten Ebene kommt man an der Anrichte, den Bädern und der Küche vorbei. In der dritten Ebene erstrecken sich das Schlafzimmer und das Wohnzimmer in ihrer ganzen Größe. Am Horizont bildet die Terrasse die vierte Ebene.

Divisé en quatre espaces qui apportent profondeur et dynamisme, cet appartement est doté d'une surface de 116 mètres carrés. Dans le premier espace, un vestibule accueille les visiteurs. Le couloir croise le garde-manger, la salle de bains et la cuisine. Dans le troisième espace, la chambre et le salon règnent par leur grandeur. Au fond, la terrasse forme le quatrième espace.

Dividido en cuatro capas espaciales que dinamizan y proporcionan profundidad, este apartamento cuenta con 116 metros cuadrados. En la primera capa, un vestíbulo recibe al visitante. El recorrido cruza la despensa, los baños y la cocina. En la tercera zona, el dormitorio y el salón reinan en su amplitud. En el horizonte, la terraza forma la cuarta capa.

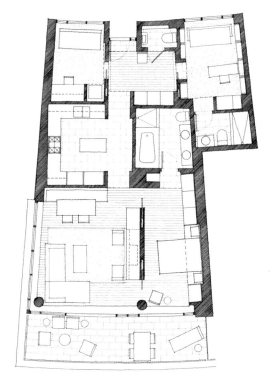

Floor plan

APARTMENT REFURBISHMENT

Íñigo Beguiristáin
Pamplona, Spain
© Iñaki Bergera

In this apartment with three bedrooms and two bathrooms, the public area is separated from the private areas with a portico with central edge beam and perimeter load-bearing walls. The use of mirrors, strategically placed to avoid reflections, visually expand the space and the swinging doors allow the different rooms to be joined or separated.

In dieser Drei-Zimmer-Wohnung mit zwei Bädern, wird der öffentliche Bereich durch ein Portal mit zentralem Randträger und tragenden Außenwänden von den privaten Bereichen getrennt. Der Einsatz von Spiegeln, strategisch so gehängt, dass keine Reflexionen entstehen, erweitert den Raum optisch und die Flügeltüren erlauben es zusätzlich, dass die unterschiedlichen Aufenthaltsräume vereint oder getrennt werden.

Dans cet appartement composé de trois pièces et deux salles de bains, la pièce commune est séparée des pièces privées par un portail de bois et des murs périmétriques. L'emploi des miroirs, stratégiquement placés pour éviter les reflets, agrandit visuellement l'espace. Les portes rabattables permettent d'unir ou de séparer les différentes pièces.

En este apartamento de tres habitaciones y dos baños, el área pública se separa de las zonas privadas mediante un pórtico con viga de borde central y muros perimetrales de carga. El uso de espejos, estratégicamente colocados para evitar reflejos, amplía visualmente el espacio, y las puertas abatibles permiten unir o separar las distintas estancias.

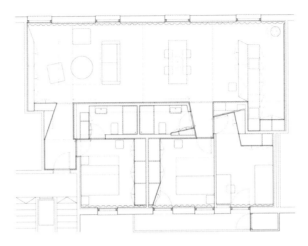

Floor plan

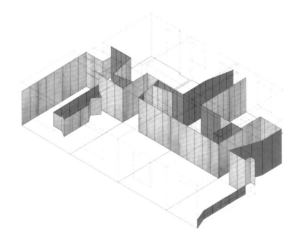

Isometric view

NEW LUXURY

Fábio Galeazzo
São Paulo, Brazil
© Rômulo Fialdini

Wood is the main protagonist in this apartment. Wooden panels cover the walls and you can glimpse the contrast between luxury and rugged materials, polished and matte surfaces, and light and dark areas. The honey-coloured dining room table is complemented by two mirrors on the wall that streamline the space with their organic form.

In diesem Apartment steht das Holz im Mittelpunkt. Holzpaneele verdecken die Wände und der Kontrast zwischen den noblen, edlen Materialien, den polierten und matten Oberflächen sowie den hellen und dunklen Bereichen, nimmt in diesem Apartment die Hauptrolle ein. Der honigfarbene Tisch des Esszimmers wird durch die Spiegel an der Wand ergänzt, welche dem Raum mit ihrer organischen Form Dynamik verleihen.

Dans cet appartement, le bois joue le rôle principal. Des panneaux de bois tapissent les murs et la décoration permet de percevoir le contraste entre les matières nobles et sauvages, les surfaces polies ou mates et les zones claires et foncées. La table de la salle à manger, de couleur miel, est complétée par deux miroirs incrustés dans la paroi de bois, ce qui dynamise le séjour avec sa forme organique.

La madera es la gran protagonista en este apartamento. Paneles de madera cubren las paredes y en la decoración se percibe el contraste entre materiales nobles y agrestes, superficies pulidas o mates y zonas claras y oscuras. La mesa del comedor, de color miel, se complementa con los dos espejos de la pared, que dinamizan la estancia con su forma orgánica.

BEACH APARTMENT

Diego Revollo
São Paulo, Brazil
© Alain Brugier

This project started with the aim of introducing a new way of understanding contemporary style. Trying to avoid falling into beach apartment stereotypes, the designers proposed a vertical garden hanging on the sea-facing facade. The white of the balcony accentuates the blue of the horizon and materials such as wood make the interior more welcoming.

Dieses Projekt entstand mit dem Ziel, eine neue Art des Verständnisses für den zeitgenössischen Stil zu schaffen. Um nicht in das Stereotyp der klassischen Ferienwohnung am Strand zu verfallen, schlugen die Designer einen vertikalen Garten vor, der von der Fassade zum Meer abgeht. Der weiße Balkon hebt das Blau des Horizonts hervor und im Innenraum bewirken Materialien wie Holz, dass es gemütlich wirkt.

Ce projet a vu le jour dans le but d'introduire une nouvelle forme de compréhension du style contemporain. En tentant de ne pas tomber dans les stéréotypes des appartements côtiers, les créateurs ont proposé un jardin vertical accroché à la façade qui donne sur la mer. Le blanc du balcon accentue le bleu de l'horizon ; à l'intérieur, les matériaux tels que le bois rendent l'appartement plus accueillant.

Este proyecto nació con el objetivo de introducir una nueva forma de entender el estilo contemporáneo. Tratando de no caer en los estereotipos de los apartamentos de playa, los diseñadores propusieron un jardín vertical que pende de la fachada que da al mar. El color blanco del balcón acentúa el azul del horizonte y, en el interior, materiales como la madera hacen que resulte más acogedor.

BASSEYNAYA STR.

Olga Akulova DESIGN
Kiev, Ukraine
© Roman Shishak

This home can be found inside a 19th century house. This is a guest apartment with a kitchen, dining room, bathroom and bedroom with a small dressing room. Pale wood parquet was used for the floor and modern style furniture was chosen. The wall of the dining room has been left bare and painted white, accentuating the idea that we are looking at an ephemeral space.

Diese Wohnung befindet sich in einem Gebäude aus dem 19. Jahrhundert. Es ist eine Gästewohnung mit Küche, Esszimmer, Badezimmer und einem Schlafzimmer mit einem kleinen Ankleideraum. Hier wurde helles Holzparkett für den Boden verwendet und dieser wurde mit modernen Designermöbeln kombiniert. Die Wand im Esszimmer blieb im Originalzustand und wurde weiß gestrichen, sie unterstreicht den Eindruck, dass man sich in einem Übergangsbereich befindet.

Cette habitation se trouve au sein d'une maison du xixe siècle. Il s'agit d'un appartement pour les invités, équipé d'une cuisine, d'une salle à manger, d'une salle de bains et d'une chambre avec petit dressing. Du parquet de bois clair a été posé au sol, et des meubles au design moderne ont été ajoutés. La cloison de la salle à manger a été ouverte et peinte en blanc, ce qui accentue l'idée d'un espace de transition.

Esta vivienda se encuentra en el interior de una casa del siglo xix. Se trata de un apartamento para invitados con cocina, comedor, baño y un dormitorio con un pequeño vestidor. Se utilizó parqué de madera clara para el suelo y muebles de diseño moderno. La pared del comedor se ha dejado a la vista y pintado de blanco, y acentúa la idea de que estamos ante un espacio transitorio.

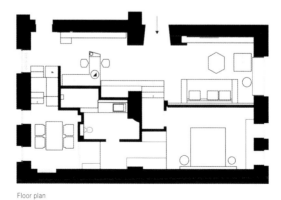

Floor plan

APARTMENT BH

Olga Akulova DESIGN
Kiev, Ukraine
© Roman Shishak

This project was based around the owners' love of the minimalist style: simple, elegant and refined. The long, hard process culminated in an apartment located in the centre of the capital city. It offers the owners a home where they can comfortably enjoy their life and at the same time, redecorating and adding new elements to the original interior design.

Dieses Projekt basiert auf der Vorliebe der Eigentümer für einen minimalistischen Stil: schlicht, elegant und raffiniert. Das Ergebnis des langen und schwierigen Umbauprozesses ist ein Apartment im Zentrum der Stadt, das seinen Eigentümern ein Zuhause bietet, in dem sie bequem das Leben genießen können und in dem sie die ursprüngliche Inneneinrichtung mit neuen Elemente dekoriert haben.

Ce projet est basé sur l'amour des propriétaires pour le style minimaliste : simple, élégant, raffiné. Le long processus a débouché sur un appartement situé au centre de la capitale, ce qui offre aux propriétaires un lieu de vie confortable. L'appartement a été redécoré et de nouveaux éléments ont été ajoutés par rapport à la décoration d'origine.

Este proyecto se basó en el amor de los propietarios por el estilo minimalista: simple, elegante y refinado. El largo y duro proceso desembocó en un apartamento situado en el centro de la capital que ofrece a sus dueños un hogar en el que disfrutar cómodamente de su vida a la vez que redecoran la vivienda y agregan nuevos elementos al interiorismo original.

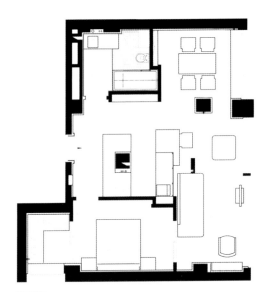

Floor plan

LOFT IN REQUENA

AreaArquitectura.Design
Valencia, Spain
© Juan David Fuertes Fotografía

This home features large, patinated-copper window frames, as well as flared shapes, white walls and naturally dark parquet flooring, all of which give the attic a modern, minimalist style. The space is functional and has been designed to harmonize with the environment, views, orientation and sunlight. The natural materials blend with the property's surroundings.

Dieses Wohnobjekt zeichnet sich durch seine großen Fenster aus patiniertem Kupfer, die sich öffnenden Formen, die weißen Wände und den natürlich dunklen Parkettboden aus, was dem Dachgeschoss einen minimalistischen und modernen Stil verleiht. Der Raum ist funktional und wurde unter Berücksichtigung der Umgebung, der Aussicht, der Ausrichtung und des Sonnenlichtes entworfen. Die natürlichen Materialien verschmelzen mit der Umgebung des Ortes.

Cette habitation se caractérise par de grandes baies vitrées en cuivre patiné, des formes évasées, des murs blancs et un parquet naturel foncé. Le tout permet de créer un style minimaliste et moderne. L'espace est fonctionnel et a été conçu d'après l'environnement, la vue, l'orientation et la lumière du soleil. Les matériaux naturels se fondent dans le décor environnant.

Esta vivienda se caracteriza por los grandes ventanales de cobre patinado, las formas abocinadas, las paredes blancas y el parqué natural oscuro, que confieren al ático un estilo minimalista y moderno. El espacio es funcional y ha sido diseñado según el entorno, las vistas, la orientación y la luz solar. Los materiales naturales se funden con los alrededores del lugar.

Floor plan

EMOTION VS REASON

Andrea Marcante, Adelaide Testa/UdA Architects
Turin, Italy
© Stefano Graziani

The remodelling of this apartment started with a town council project that promotes the conversion of industrial buildings; for this reason recycled materials and furniture have been used. Inhabited by a young couple, this home swings between the rationality of its architecture and the emotive nature of the furnishings that complement it.

Der Umbau dieses Apartments ist Teil eines von der Stadt geförderten Projekts zur Renovierung alter Industriegebäude. Aus diesem Grund hat man die ursprünglichen Materialien und Möbelstücke wieder aufbereitet und verwendet. Bewohnt wird das Apartment von einem jungen Paar und es ist eine spannende Mischung zwischen der Rationalität seiner Architektur und der Emotionalität der eingesetzten Möbel.

Cet appartement a été rénové suite à un projet du maire de la ville, qui encourageait la rénovation des bâtiments industriels ; c'est pourquoi certains matériaux et pièces de mobilier ont été réutilisés. Un jeune couple vit dans cet appartement, où la rationalité de l'architecture le dispute au caractère émotionnel des meubles qu'il accueille.

La reforma de este apartamento parte de un proyecto del ayuntamiento de la ciudad que promueve la renovación de edificios industriales; por este motivo se han reutilizado materiales y piezas de mobiliario. Habitada por una joven pareja, la vivienda se debate entre la racionalidad de su arquitectura y la emotividad de los muebles que la complementan.

First floor plan

Second floor plan

PENTHOUSE G

Architekten LEE+MIR
Bayern, Germany
© Christina Kratzenberg

In a military zone, this 150 m² attic with terrace offers its owners a space where they can live in luxury and comfort. This home, with its spacious rooms, large windows and skylights is flooded with natural light during the day. Made-to-measure furniture has been designed by the interior design studio.

Dieses 150 m² große Penthaus mit Terrasse liegt in einem Militärbereich und bietet seinen Eigentümern einen luxuriösen und komfortablen Lebensraum. Die Wohnung hat große Räume, riesige Fenster und Oberlichter, durch die tagsüber natürliches Licht hineinscheint. Das handgefertigte Mobiliar wurde vom Innendesignstudio entworfen.

Situé dans une zone militaire, cet attique de 150 m² avec terrasse offre à ses propriétaires un lieu de vie confortable et luxueux. La journée, cette habitation aux pièces spacieuses et aux grandes baies vitrées est inondée de lumière. Le mobilier, fabriqué sur mesure, a été conçu par l'architecte d'intérieur.

Emplazado en un área de uso militar, este ático de 150 m² con terraza ofrece a sus propietarios un espacio para vivir de un modo lujoso y confortable. Esta vivienda, de habitaciones espaciosas, grandes ventanales y claraboyas, se inunda de luz natural durante el día. El mobiliario, fabricado a medida, ha sido diseñado por el estudio interiorista.

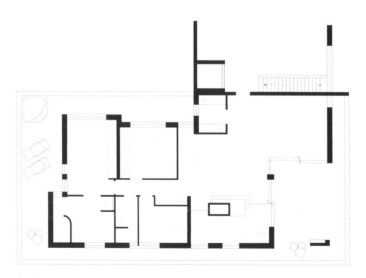

Floor plan

SANT PERE 47

Miguel Ángel Borrás, Elodie Grammont/MIEL ARQUITECTOS
Barcelona, Spain
© Nuria Vila

The remodelling of this home is a reinterpretation of a typical 19th century apartment in Eixample, Barcelona. Two golden rails follow the line of the walls and conceal wiring and lighting within them, as well as bearing the weight of the doors and a sliding ladder. Storage spaces have been installed in the extra space above the rails.

Der Umbau dieser Wohnung ist eine räumliche Neuinterpretation einer typischen Wohnung eines Stadtteils in Barcelona aus dem 19. Jahrhundert. Zwei goldene Leisten folgen der Kontinuität der Wände und verdecken in ihrem Inneren die Kabel und die Beleuchtung, während sie gleichzeitig das Gewicht der Türen und eine verschiebbare Treppe tragen. Im Extra-Raum, oberhalb der Leisten, wurden Stauräume eingerichtet.

La rénovation de cette habitation est une relecture spatiale de l'appartement typique de l'agrandissement de Barcelone au XIXe siècle. Deux lignes dorées suivent la continuité des murs et cachent les câbles et l'éclairage, tout en supportant le poids des portes et une échelle. Les combles et des espaces de rangement occupent l'espace supplémentaire situé au-dessus de l'appartement.

La reforma de esta vivienda es una relectura espacial del típico piso del Ensanche barcelonés del siglo XIX. Dos guías doradas siguen la continuidad de las paredes y esconden, en su interior, el cableado y la iluminación, a la vez que soportan el peso de puertas y una escalera deslizante. En el espacio extra que queda por encima de las guías se han colocado altillos y espacios de almacenaje.

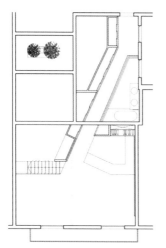

Second floor plan

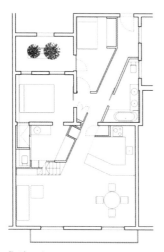

First floor plan

ROBINSON CASA

Another Design International
Hong Kong, China
© Virgile Simon Bertrand

This 200 m² apartment is in the middle of the big city. The architect, of Chinese origin, absorbed international design influences to create a unique concept that blends the best elements of Eastern and Western traditions. The result is a home, where most of the walls have been removed, reserving a private area for the owner.

Mitten in der Großstadt trifft man auf dieses 200 m² große Apartment. Der chinesische Architekt ließ sich von internationalen Designs inspirieren und schaffte ein einzigartiges Konzept, das das Beste aus den Traditionen des Orients und des Okzidents vereint. Das Ergebnis ist eine Wohnung, aus der man den größten Teil der Wände entfernt hat und in der der Eigentümer dennoch einen Privatbereich erhält.

Cet appartement de 200 m² est situé au cœur de cette grande ville. L'architecte, d'origine chinoise, puise dans les influences internationales pour créer un concept unique qui mêle les meilleurs éléments des traditions orientales et occidentales. Il en résulte une habitation dans laquelle la plupart des cloisons ont été supprimées, tout en préservant une partie privée réservée au propriétaire.

En medio de la gran ciudad se encuentra este apartamento de 200 m². El arquitecto, de origen chino, bebe de las influencias del diseño internacional para crear un concepto único que mezcla los mejores elementos de las tradiciones de Oriente y Occidente. El resultado es una vivienda en la que se ha eliminado la mayor parte de las paredes, reservando un área privada para el propietario.

LOFT IN BROOKLYN

James Slade
www.sladearch.com

Since the owner is in retail the apartment follows more of a retail strategy than a traditional living space might. Ground floor is living dining, second is two girls bedrooms with a shared lounge between them and a study off to the side, top floor is owner's bedroom and study with a sneaker wall to display his very large collection of sneakers.

Le propriétaire étant dans le commerce de détail, ce loft suit une stratégie plus commerciale qu'un espace de vie traditionnel. Le rez-de-chaussée est consacré au séjour et aux repas, le premier étage aux deux chambres, qui se partagent un salon, sans compter le bureau sur le côté. Au niveau supérieur, avec la chambre du père et son bureau, un mur tout entier est dédié à son collection de baskets.

Dass der Bauherr im Einzelhandel tätig ist, schlägt sich auch in der Gestaltung seiner Wohnung wieder. Auf der Ebene des Erdgeschosses sind die Bereiche Wohnen und Essen zu finden, darüber befinden sich die Schlafzimmer der beiden Töchter mit einem dazwischen liegenden Gemeinschaftsraum und einem Arbeitszimmer an einer Seite. Auf der obersten Ebene liegt das Schlafzimmer des Eigentümers und sein Büro mit einer Wand, die seiner riesigen Turnschuhsammlung gewidmet ist.

De eigenaar werkt in de detailhandel en dat is terug te zien in de opzet van deze woonruimte. De begane grond is voor slapen en wonen, op de eerste verdieping zijn twee meisjesslaapkamers met een hal ertussen en een werkkamer opzij, en de bovenste verdieping bevat de slaapkamer en werkkamer van de eigenaar en een wand voor zijn enorme collectie sneakers.

El apartamento, propiedad de un vendedor, sigue más las directrices de un local comercial que las de una vivienda tradicional. En la primera planta hay un salón y un comedor; en la segunda, dos dormitorios con una sala y un estudio, y en la planta superior se encuentran el dormitorio y el despacho del propietario, con una amplia colección de zapatillas deportivas.

Dal momento che il proprietario è un commerciante, questo appartamento segue un criterio adatto a un locale atto alla vendita al dettaglio più che alla vita quotidiana. Al pianterreno si trova la sala da pranzo, al secondo due camere da letto, un salotto e uno studio; all'ultimo piano è stata prevista la camera da letto del proprietario e uno studio con un'ampia collezione di scarpe da tennis.

Dado que o proprietário trabalha na área da venda a retalho, o apartamento segue mais uma estratégia de retalho do que de um espaço tradicional de habitação. O rés-de-chão é sala de jantar e de estar; o primeiro andar tem dois quartos com uma sala comum e um gabinete; o andar superior é o quarto do proprietário, havendo ainda uma sala com uma parede de exposição para sapatos de desporto.

På grund av innehavarens verksamhet inom detaljhandeln präglas våningen kanske i högre grad än andra bostäder av en kommersiell anda. Bottenplanet inrymmer allrum/matplats, andra våningsplanet inrymmer sovrum för två fl ickor med ett mellanliggande gemensamt rum och arbetsrum i fil. Översta våningen inrymmer ägarens sovrum och arbetsrum med en vägg som presenterar hans stora samling gymnastikskor.

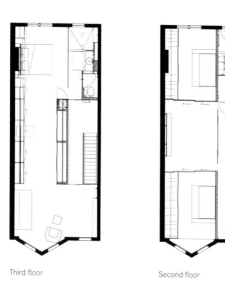

Third floor

Second floor

Ground floor

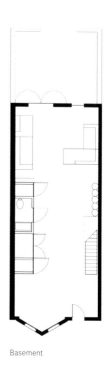

Basement

LOFT IN PASSATGE SERT

Sara Folch
www.sarafolch.com

The building where this loft is located is a former textile factory designed by the architect Sert. The original building structure has been maintained but the interior reformed to create a number of lofts. The design idea is clear: to generate various diaphanous spaces separated but integrated in turn within a whole.

L'immeuble où est installé ce loft est une ancienne usine textile construite par l'architecte Josep Lluís Sert. Si l'ossature d'origine a survécu, l'intérieur a été remanié pour héberger un certain nombre de lofts. Les rénovateurs avaient un objectif évident, celui de générer des espaces lumineux, séparés, mais intégrés dans un tout.

Dieses Loft befindet sich im Gebäude einer ehemaligen Textilfabrik, die von Josep Lluís Sert entworfen wurde. Die Originalstruktur des Gebäudes blieb erhalten, doch im Inneren wurden mehrere Lofts eingerichtet. Die zugrunde liegende Idee bestand darin, mehrere offene Räume zu schaffen, die voneinander getrennt sind und doch zu einem Ganzen zusammenfinden.

Het gebouw waarin deze loft zich bevindt, is een voormalige textielfabriek ontworpen door de architect Sert. De structuur van het gebouw is gehandhaafd, maar het interieur is verbouwd om enkele lofts te creëren. Het idee achter het ontwerp is duidelijk: meerdere transparante ruimten in het leven roepen die gescheiden zijn maar toch een geheel vormen.

La finca donde está ubicado este loft es una antigua fábrica textil realizada por el arquitecto Josep Lluís Sert. La estructura original del edificio se ha mantenido, pero su interior ha sido reformado creando varios loft. La idea del proyecto era clara: generar varios espacios diáfanos separados pero integrados a su vez en un todo.

L'area su cui sorge questo loft è una vecchia fabbrica tessile progettata dall'architetto Sert. La struttura originale dell'edificio è stata conservata, ma gli interni sono stati ristrutturati creando diversi loft. L'idea del progetto era chiara: generare vari spazi diafani separati, ma nel contempo integrati in un insieme.

O edifício no qual se situa este loft é uma antiga fábrica têxtil concebida pelo arquiteto Sert. A estrutura original do edifício foi mantida, mas o interior foi renovado com o fim de criar uma série de lofts. A ideia de design é clara: criar vários espaços diáfanos separados, mas integrados num todo.

Den byggnad i vilken loftvåningen inryms är en äldre textilfabrik ritad av arkitekten Josep Lluís Sert. Byggnadens ursprungliga stomme har behållits, men interiören har renoverats och omorganiserats till ett flertal loftvåningar. Projektidén var tydlig: att skapa ljusa genomsynliga rum separerade från varandra men samtidigt förenade genom en övergripande enhetlighet.

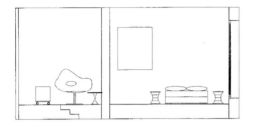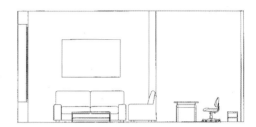

Sections

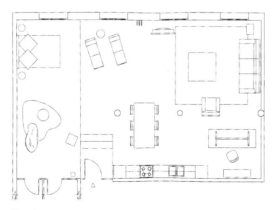

Floor plan

LOFT EN CAMPS ELISIS

GCA Arquitectes
www.gcaarq.com

This loft is located in a home on the ground floor of a building that comprises a ground and first floor. Conceived for a couple, it follows a simple and industrial design idea, using basic building materials with no concession to adornment, with the result based on the rigor of the architecture.

Ce loft est situé au rez-de-chaussée d'un bâtiment d'un étage. Conçu pour un couple, il suit un concept industriel simple et se sert des matériaux de construction sans faire de concessions ornementales, d'où un résultat fondé sur la rigueur de l'architecture.

Dieses Loft liegt im Erdgeschoss eines einstöckigen Wohnhauses. Es ist für ein Paar entworfen und in einem einfachen, industriell inspirierten Design gehalten. Unter Verzicht auf jegliches schmückendes Beiwerk wurden nur grundlegende Baumaterialien verwendet, sodass die Architektur hier die Hauptrolle spielt.

Deze loft bevindt zich in een huis op de parterre van een gebouw met een begane grond en een eerste verdieping. Hij is ontworpen voor een paar, volgt een eenvoudig en industrieel ontwerp waarvoor basale bouwmaterialen zijn gebruikt zonder concessies te doen aan decoratie. Het resultaat berust op de striktheid van de architectuur.

Este loft está situado en el piso superior de un edificio de dos plantas. Pensado como vivienda para una pareja, se creó un diseño sencillo de carácter industrial, utilizando materiales de construcción básicos, sin concesiones al adorno, basando el resultado en el rigor de la arquitectura.

Questo loft si trova in un'abitazione che occupa il primo piano di un edificio formato da pianterreno e primo piano. Il progetto, pensato per una coppia, sorge da un'idea semplice e industriale, utilizzando materiali edili di base, senza concedere nulla alla decorazione, e poggiando il risultato sul rigore dell'architettura.

Este loft situa-se numa casa no rés-de-chão de um edifício que inclui um rés-de-chão e um primeiro andar. Concebido para um casal, segue uma ideia de design simples e industrial, utilizando materiais de construção básicos sem pensar em embelezamento e tendo como resultado o rigor da arquitetura.

Denna loftvåning är inrymd på nedre plan i ett tvåplanshus. Våningen avsedd för två personer har formgivits utifrån en tanke om enkelhet och industriell prägel utan excesser baserat på grundläggande byggnadsmaterial. Slutresultatet återspeglar en konsekvent arkitektur.

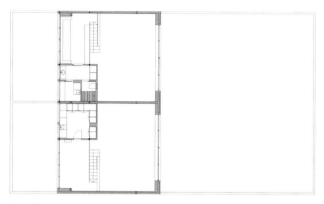

Second floor

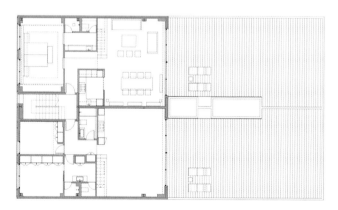

Ground floor